14 Days of Agape

Rosilind Jukić

www.rosilindjukic.com

Updated 2015 with Bible study materials and printable verses

All Scripture verses are taken from the New King James version of the Holy Bible.

Table of Contents

Introduction

It's called the "love chapter". Couples often refer to its verses at their weddings, romantic greeting cards quote its truths, and we often reflect on how we can apply it to our marriages (or wish our spouses were more like what these verses declare love to be).

Over the next 14 chapters I would like to throw a different perspective on 1 Corinthians 13 - from romance to relationship.

A simple glance at the Greek word used for love in this chapter enlightens us to the fact that Paul was not talking about love in the context of marriage. This book was a letter written as a letter of instruction to a church in the town of Corinth. Thus, we must approach this chapter from that standpoint. Obviously, the truths in this passage can and should be applied to marriage - but they should also be applied to every other relationship in life.

Since the book of 1 Corinthians was directed to a congregation, I took 14 days to blog about it from the perspective of the church - our relationship with our brothers and sisters in Christ - and how this passage can and should be applied to our church family.

The idea to blog through 1 Corinthians 13 began toward the end of 2012. As over the next two months I meditated on the message of this chapter, God began to slowly reveal to me a new aspect of its message. I sat down several times during that time to prepare each blog post ahead of time, which is my usual practice, but the words never came. In the end, I blogged each day for 14 days – something I have never done in 9 years of blogging! Although it was not easy, I found that it deepened the experience for me in ways I never imagined. The topics of love, faith, grace, hope, and perfect kindness were on my mind and in my heart each day as I woke up, opened my Bible and meditated on the verse I planned to blog about that day. Many times over those 14 days I would find myself responding in a manner that did not display agape love, and was forced to reexamine my attitude and align it to what I was learning.

Those 14 days truly changed my perspective on so many aspects of love, local church, and my relationship to the body of Christ. I pray that this message will speak to your heart as well – as together we strive to extend the perfect love of God to a world in need!

— *Rosilind Jukić*

Introductory Study Materials

Write out today's verse *1 John 4:7-8:*

_____

_____

_____

_____

_____

Write down the keywords in this verse:

_____   _____

_____   _____

_____   _____

_____   _____

_____   _____

_____   _____

What does this verse mean for your personal life right now? In what way can you put it to practical use?

_____

_____

_____

_____

_____

To whom was the book of 1 Corinthians written? _____

So, we can conclude that the context of love in this chapter is addressing whom? _____

Where does love come from? _____

What does this mean to you? _____

How can we know we're born of God? _____

If we don't show love to those around us, what does it mean? _____

1 John 4 doesn't say that God loves or that God shows love. John does not use an action verb, he doesn't use "love" as a direct object; rather he uses the "be" verb "is". This indicates that love is the very character of God. It is *who He is!* Share your thoughts about this below:

_____

_____

_____

_____

_____

Notes

A Beautiful Tongue of Gold

"Though I speak with the tongues of men and of angels, but have not love, I have become sounding brass or a clanging cymbal." 1 Corinthians 13:1

The tongue has been a very damaging element in many churches all over the world.

It speaks gossip and slander.

It is critical and invites negativity.

It divides and cuts.

It damages, discourages and demeans.

James tells us that it has the power of life or death. And sadly, it brings more death than life.

Paul says that though we may be an eloquent speaker and have ability to mesmerize people with our ability to paint masterpieces with our words, while we may enlighten the masses to the mysteries of God's Word like no other or speak the language of supernatural beings if it is not done in *love* it is just noise.

Paul actually uses the terms "sounding brass" and "clanging cymbal".

Clanging.

This is somewhat synonymous with irritating or annoying. Irritating tongues of brass that have lost their value and beauty.

There was a time in my life when I criticized Christian leaders and spoke negatively about God's church - I often proclaimed it backslidden, cold and void of God's presence.

Perhaps some of the things I said were technically correct, but they didn't come from a heart of love. They came from a negative and critical spirit that was self-righteous and filled with pride.

It's not so much *what* we say as much as what is in our heart when we say it. If what we say does not spring from a fountain of love that seeks to build up and unify God's church, if more than 50% of what we speak is criticism and negativity, we need to fall on our knees and ask the Holy Spirit to fill us with *His* l*ove* so that our words have value and beauty, so that they are easily received and bring forth fruit in the lives of the hearer.

May our tongues be beautiful tongues of gold, filled with God's love - Agape love!

But what does *love* mean? Many a meddling Christian has spoken death under the guise of "speaking the truth in love." This is exactly what we will be exploring over the next 13 chapters.

How can we be sure that we are using our tongue to bring life to Christ's body?

How can we be certain we are building it up and not tearing it down?

How can we unify and edify His family better?

This chapter is rich with truths that can answer all of these questions and more.

I hope you join me in digging and exploring this wonderful and life-building passage from God's Word!

Day 1 Study Materials

Write out today's verse *1 Corinthians 13:1:*

_____

_____

_____

_____

_____

Write down the keywords in this verse:

_____   _____

_____   _____

_____   _____

_____   _____

_____   _____

What does this verse mean for your personal life right now? In what way can you put it to practical use?

_____

_____

_____

_____

_____

How can we be sure that we are using our tongue to bring life to Christ's body?

_____

_____

_____

_____

_____

How can we be certain we are building it up and not tearing it down?

_____

_____

_____

_____

_____

How can we unify and edify His family better?

_____

_____

_____

_____

_____

Have you used your tongue lately as a tool or as a weapon? _____

List 3 things you can do to use your tongue to build up and not tear down

Write James 3 below and then circle the parts that stand out to you most.

Write out a prayer below to the Lord to help you use your tongue as an encouragement to your brothers and sisters in the Lord.

_____

_____

_____

_____

_____

_____

_____

_____

_____

_____

_____

_____

_____

_____

_____

_____

_____

_____

_____

_____

_____

Notes

I Want to Be Somebody

"And though I have [the gift of] prophecy, and understand all mysteries and all knowledge, and though I have all faith, so that I could remove mountains, but have not love, I am nothing." 1 Corinthians 13:2

He had made the mistake of choosing to ignore God the first time. The consequences were devastating. I am sure we can all relate to that, at one point or another. God has interesting and often times painful ways of getting our attention, and for Jonah it was no different. Just put yourself in his place for a moment.

After being vomited up on shore, which in itself was no pleasant experience, he chose to obey God and carry the prophetic word God had given him to the city of Nineveh. The prophetic word was to repent or suffer God's judgment. He did and the whole city fasted, prayed and repented. And God chose not to judge them. But Jonah was unhappy.

Why?

Because he ***wanted*** to see the city judged. He was actually angry and said, "I ***knew*** this would happen!"

Yes, he was angry with God! He even wanted to die, he was so angry!

And I often ask myself: *What kind of a prophet would deliver a message from God to a wicked city, calling them to repentance and then get angry when they repent?*

But we are that way at times. We see a brother or sister in sin, we pray for their repentance, and perhaps even confront them. Then they repent ***and*** are very blessed of the Lord and we grow bitter because what we ***really*** wanted was for them to experience God's judgment.

In other words, we wanted to rejoice in their downfall. *(If we are downright honest about it)*

But Paul told us that we could have the gift of prophecy - like Jonah - and even have great understanding of all scriptures mysteries and knowledge about God's Word. We might say that this is a very discerning person. We can even have great faith - so much that we can even move mountains *(and that, my friends, is amazing faith)*.

Just pause for a moment and consider what kind of Christian this would be:

A prophet.

A person who can interpret scripture excellently and discern situations and types of people.

A person who understands the hidden mysteries of scripture - likely one who "gets" those prophetic books (a wheel in a wheel, anyone?) and can deliver that message in an understandable way.

A person of amazing and powerful faith.

This is Mr. Super Christian!

But without **love** he is **nothing**.

NOTHING!

The Bible actually says he is ***NOTHING***.

All of the prophecies in the world, all of the knowledge and faith He has given to us to share with others will amount to less than a hill of beans if we do not have love. *God's message to His people must always be packaged with love!*

Jonah did not carry God's message with love. He was judgmental, critical and self-righteous. God relented and had mercy and grace on Nineveh, and that angered Jonah to the point of suicide, because as God's messenger he was *nothing.*

I love how we see that God's heart was about the people. His mercy and grace was not dependent upon the messenger, but the people who heard the message. His message was heard and obeyed, even though Jonah didn't share it in love. The person whom this hurt the most was the carrier.

But this is not always the case. Oftentimes everyone is affected by the fact that we share God's message in pride, self-righteousness and anger. Sometimes this can carry devastating consequences of division and broken relationships. This is *never* God's will for His church.

Has God planted a message in your heart? Has He spoken to you a word to share with a brother or sister? Before you share it, get down on your knees and pray for a heart of love. Examine your own heart and motives before you share this message. And then pray that it will be received with an open heart of joy, and that it will bring forth much fruit in the heart of the listener!

Day 2 Study Materials

Write out today's verse *1 Corinthians 13:2:*

_____

_____

_____

_____

_____

Write down the keywords in this verse:

_____   _____

_____   _____

_____   _____

_____   _____

_____   _____

What does this verse mean for your personal life right now? In what way can you put it to practical use?

_____

_____

_____

_____

_____

Why was Jonah depressed? _____

What negative qualities do we display when we fail to mingle love with prophesy, understanding, knowledge, and faith?

_____

_____

_____

_____

_____

_____

Why do you think this is?

_____

_____

_____

_____

How do you think the church would be transformed, and how do you think our effectiveness would change, if we would do better at allowing love to influence our prophesies, understanding, knowledge and faith?

_____

_____

_____

_____

_____

_____

_____

Notes

Have You Sacrificed It All In Vain?

"And though I bestow all my goods to feed [the poor], and though I give my body to be burned, but have not love, it profits me nothing." 1 Corinthians 13:3

Some of my greatest idols are missionaries. They truly obeyed Jesus' words and left family, home, and possessions; they went to a place so unfamiliar with a culture so foreign to all they'd ever known. Some lived in near poverty. Others buried wives and children in foreign soil.

Their stories are captivating and their sacrifice astounding. Reading stories like these convicts us and perhaps even motivates us to be more sacrificial in our own lives. Truly, all of us could learn to live more humbly and sacrificially. We can do with much less than what we rely on now. Sometimes its simply a matter of lowering our standard of living to become a blessing to others.

Even more captivating are stories of martyrs who gave their very lives for Christ; who refused to back down in face of mortal danger and gave their very bodies to ensure the message of the gospel reached across oceans and lands, years and generations - to ultimately reach you and me. Their stories are gruesome at times but their sacrifice selfless and endearing.

And yet, Paul reminds us in 1 Corinthians 13:3 that we can sacrifice our possessions to feed and clothe the poor, or even our own bodies to save another, but if it is not done with love - God's love, a love that doesn't come with ultimatums or strings attached, then we did it all in vain.

Imagine giving your most loved and prized possession - even your own life - only to find out later that your sacrifice was entirely in vain! All we do, all we say, every attitude of our heart and every breath we breathe must be bathed and saturated in love.

My dear friends, if we want our works for the kingdom of God to have value, if we want our lives to count for something, if we want to receive a reward from God's hand, we must allow His love to saturate every part of us: body, soul and spirit. If we don't, nothing we do has value, we will be nothing and all be in vain.

Dear friends, do you want to know what God's love looks like? Starting tomorrow we will begin looking at each element of Agape - God's kind of love.

Day 3 Study Materials

Write out today's verse *1 Corinthians 13:3:*

_____

_____

_____

_____

_____

Write down the keywords in this verse:

_____   _____

_____   _____

_____   _____

_____   _____

_____   _____

_____   _____

What does this verse mean for your personal life right now? In what way can you put it to practical use?

_____

_____

_____

_____

_____

Why do you think Paul says that sacrifice without love is meaningless?

_____

_____

_____

_____

_____

_____

How can we put this verse into the context of the 21st century?

_____

_____

_____

_____

_____

_____

List 5 ways you can show sacrificial love to someone this week

_____

_____

_____

_____

_____

Now, write out a plan of action to remind yourself to do these 5 things this week

_____

_____

Notes

5 Elements That Build or Destroy the Church

"Love suffers long [and] is kind; love does not envy; love does not parade itself, is not puffed up;" 1 Corinthians 13:4

What is love? True love? What is the kind of love God wants us to have for His body, His church, our brothers and sisters in Christ?

I would dare to say that I have met very few people who display what we read about in 1 Corinthians 13. These are areas I am working on in my own life and I pray that each day I am more mature in true love than the day before.

1. *It suffers long.*

We all know *that* person. The one who has the gift for saying the wrong thing at the wrong time. The one who makes Eyore appear giddy. The one who has the tendency to annoy, dominate conversations, or has more idiosyncrasies than the average bear.

Agape love does not just tolerate these precious people. It doesn't marginalize them or even allow itself to focus on their short-comings. Agape love remembers that we, too, have short-comings and probably have our own habits that annoy and irritate.

No, agape love openly accepts and embraces these people - faults and all. It remembers that these, too, have a place in building God's Kingdom. It is patient with them and ultimately and lovingly challenges them to grow to be more like Christ!

2. *It is kind.*

Agape love remembers the hurting, the sick, the shut-ins, the grieving widow and widower who have to somehow cope without the one who shared in their joys and sorrows, good and bad.

It reaches out to the one who tends to get left behind and embraces the "prickly" character that others tend to avoid. Agape love refuses to listen to anything negative about its brothers and sisters, but keeps the spotlight focused on their good qualities.

3. *It doesn't envy.*

Agape love doesn't view others' successes as a threat to its own success, nor does it view others' possessions as a threat to its security and sense of self worth; because it is not owned by anything and doesn't seek to get ahead.

Agape love actually *wants* others to get ahead and even be better than himself. And it truly wants others to have their hearts desires, even when that desire is something they've always wanted.

4. *It doesn't boast.*

Agape love doesn't seek the spotlight, so it has no reason to be ostentatious. Whatever it has, any success it has attained, any degree it has earned, or any position it fills is merely a gift from God and therefore it has no reason to parade itself as if it these achievements have personal merit.

However, Agape love doesn't not diminish these gifts of God as if they are nothing. It doesn't seek to diminish its own value either. If given opportunity to come to the forefront, it will neither broadcast it nor turn it down.

Agape love is not preoccupied with itself at all! It neither thinks too much or too little of itself. Rather, it has the ability to see itself through the lens of reality: that we all have value because we are created in God's image. Anything we have or achieved - even by our own hard work - is a gift of God and doesn't not increase our worth or value in God's eyes.

5. *It is not puffed up.*

Because Agape love is not preoccupied with itself nor does it have an inflated view of itself, but rather has the ability to see itself through the prism of true worth and value, it will never behave arrogantly toward another. It has not allowed its successes, education or achievements to give him the impression that he is somehow better, nor does he believe his own "press reports".

Agape love rejects pride and arrogance, remembering that these are mortal danger in the life of a Christian - for they are the very reasons why Satan himself was cast out of Heaven.

He also remembers that God rejects the proud. He routinely allows the Lord to shine His purifying light into his heart to reveal any areas of pride or arrogance, so he may be able to receive the full measure of God's grace *(for God gives grace to the humble)*.

This true humility *(as described in the area of not being boastful),* frees us to embrace our brothers and sisters with genuine and sincere love and extend God's grace to them in all situations: when they succeed and when they fail.

Dear reader, these 5 elements of love are not only necessary to the life of the believer, they are vital for building God's kingdom on earth. We cannot truly build God's kingdom if we do not have these 5 elements of love actively growing and operating in our lives. Because anything opposite of them will hinder and literally kill the work God wants to do in and through us.

My prayer today is that I walk in true Agape love among my brothers and sisters in Christ - and in those areas where I am weak, that He will strengthen me and cause me to grow and mature in love!

Day 4 Study Materials

Write out today's verse *1 Corinthians 13:4:*

_____

_____

_____

_____

_____

Write down the keywords in this verse:

_____   _____

_____   _____

_____   _____

_____   _____

_____   _____

What does this verse mean for your personal life right now? In what way can you put it to practical use?

_____

_____

_____

_____

_____

Rate yourself in these areas on a scale of 1-10, 1 = This does not describe me at all and 10 = this describes me very well.

Suffers long _____   Doesn't boast _____
Kind _____   Not puffed up _____
Doesn't envy_____

Now, have your spouse or close friend rate these areas in your life

Suffers long _____   Doesn't boast _____
Kind _____   Not puffed up _____
Doesn't envy_____

List 3 ways you could improve in these five areas

Suffers long

_____
_____
_____

Kind

_____
_____
_____

Doesn't envy

_____
_____
_____

Doesn't boast

_____
_____
_____

Not puffed up

_____

_____

_____

How do you think the church would be transformed if the body of Christ consistently displayed these qualities?

_____

_____

_____

_____

_____

_____

_____

_____

In what way can *you* influence your local church positively in these areas?

_____

_____

_____

_____

_____

_____

_____

_____

_____

_____

_____

_____

Notes

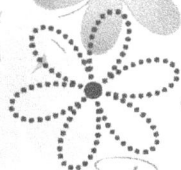

Beloved, let us love one another, for love is of God; and everyone who loves is born of God and knows God. eloved, let us love one another, for love is of God; and everyone who loves is born of God and knows God.

1 John 4:7-8

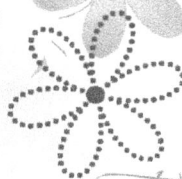

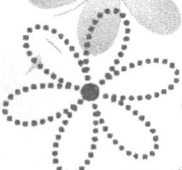

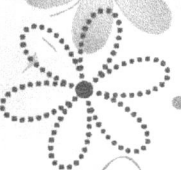

Though I speak with the tongues of men and of angels, but have not love, I have become sounding brass or a clanging cymbal.

1 Corinthians 13:1

And though I have the gift of prophecy, and understand all mysteries and all knowledge, and though I have all faith, so that I could remove mountains, but have not love, I am nothing. have not love, it profits me nothing.

1 Corinthians 13:2

And though I bestow all my goods to feed the poor, and though I give my body to be burned, but have not love, it profits me nothing.

1 Corinthians 13:3

Love suffers long and is kind; love does not envy; love does not parade itself, is not puffed up

1 Corinthians 13:4

You Had Better Hang On To That Piece of Your Mind – You Might Need It

"does not behave rudely," 1 Corinthians 13:5a

We have all experienced those times when we were engaged in a heated conflict and the *perfect* Oscar-worthy, sarcasm-dripping comeback graced our mind and we were presented with a choice:

1. Speak it and relive the glory of that *perfect moment* for days to come or

2. Choose grace *(which sounds a lot less exciting)*.

However, agape love - Jesus' perfect love - does not behave rudely. It is perfect grace even in the face of the unmannerly. This doesn't mean we become a doormat and just let people tread all over us. There are times when we *must* respond to those who do not display agape love to let them know that they may not behave unseemly toward us, but those moments must still be covered and saturated in God's love. Because when you respond to rude behavior with rude behavior, you lose your testimony.

May we never forget that there is a world of critics out there who are ready to pounce on Christians not portraying Christ. Jesus said that the world would know that we are disciples by the love we show for one another. He wasn't talking about sappy, saccharine-laced conversations sprinkled with *God bless you* or *Hallelujah.* Jesus was talking about when we are under pressure and are tempted to lose our cool, and we decide to employ discipline and guard our mouths when others would give the other person a piece of their mind they can ill afford to part with – *that's* when the world will recognize that we have something *more.* Something *desirable.* Something *needful!*

Dear reader, I wish I could say that I have this in perfect operation in my own life. But I don't. I have failed so many times! But I can say that I am much better today than I used to be. One thing that has helped me tremendously is, when I am aware that I have behaved rudely (or even just responded wrongly to a comment or situation), to contact that person and apologize. It's not easy - in fact, it is downright humiliating! But it has taught me to reflect a little before allowing sarcastic statements, harsh words, or frustration seep through.
I pray that over this next year I'll be even better at grace and love than I am today!

Day 5 Study Materials

Write out today's verse *1 Corinthians 13:5a:*

_____

_____

_____

_____

_____

Write down the keywords in this verse:

_____   _____

_____   _____

_____   _____

_____   _____

_____   _____

_____   _____

What does this verse mean for your personal life right now? In what way can you put it to practical use?

_____

_____

_____

_____

_____

The Greek word for "rudely" literally means unbecoming or disgraceful; describe a time when you perhaps behaved in such a way toward a brother or sister in Christ.

_____

_____

_____

_____

_____

Have you resolved this issue? _____

If not, is there a way to resolve this issue and what steps do you need to take to do that?

_____

_____

_____

_____

_____

Write out James 4:1

_____

_____

List 3 ways believers can learn to bring their "desires for pleasure" under control so that our behavior to one another becomes us.

_____

_____

_____

Notes

We Do Not Have Rights to Entitlements

"does not seek its own," 1 Corinthians 13:5b

We hear so much about rights: gun rights, gay rights, abortion rights, religious rights, human rights. It's all about entitlement. Young people are have an entitlement to an education, families have an entitlement to health insurance and affordable healthcare, the elderly have an entitlement to Medicare and Social Security, and the impoverished and unemployed have an entitlement to assistance.

Yet Paul said something that is very revolutionary: *Agape love doesn't seek its own rights.*

We see this grasping for rights in our churches as well. *"I have a right to have my pastor visit me when I'm ill." "I have a right to have my brothers and sisters contact me during the week." "I have a right to have the worship leader sing the songs I like."*

Growing up as a pastor's kid I watched many Christians draw the battle lines over their rights - and have drawn a few as well. But imagine for a moment a church more concerned about meeting needs than standing up for their personal rights. This is not a utopia; this is what God created the church to be. We will never be salt and light to the world as Jesus commanded as long as we are entrenched in a war for our rights. Until we are prepared to surrender our personal rights and accept our responsibility to meet the needs of those we call "brother" and "sister", and until we are ready to meet the needs of the lost souls God longs to send us, we will never truly be the church in the sense that God intended.

Agape love is more concerned about personal responsibility than personal rights. Agape love lays down the right to have the pastor visit when she is ill, and accepts her responsibility to pray daily for her pastor and church leaders. It lays down the right to expect her brothers and sisters contact her during the week and accepts her responsibility to reach out them first and meet any needs they may have! It lays down her right to have the worship leader sing the songs she likes and accepts her responsibility to come to God's house each week with a heart to worship God with her whole being in spirit and in truth.

Are you engaged in a battle for your rights?

Paul also said this: "Let nothing be done through selfish ambition or conceit, but in lowliness of mind let each esteem others better than himself. Let each of you look out not only for his own interests, but also for the interests of others." Philippians 2:3

There are three things you can do to begin practicing Agape love. Make a list of personal rights you know you ought to surrender, let your anger and frustration serve as a reminder that there is a personal right you haven't yet surrendered, and memorize the above passage as a reminder that love does not seek its own.

Day 6 Study Materials

Write out today's verse *1 Corinthians 13:5b:*

_____

_____

_____

_____

_____

Write down the keywords in this verse:

_____   _____

_____   _____

_____   _____

_____   _____

_____   _____

_____   _____

What does this verse mean for your personal life right now? In what way can you put it to practical use?

_____

_____

_____

_____

_____

Make a list of those things you feel you have a right to, concerning your local church.

_____

_____

_____

_____

_____

Now, take each of those rights and find a way to turn them into a personal responsibility, as I illustrated in the chapter above.

_____

_____

_____

_____

_____

Write out Philippians 2:3

_____

_____

_____

_____

Paul said to look out for the interests of others. In what way can your begin reaching out to those in your local body to bless them and show them that you esteem them and their needs higher than your own?

_____

_____

_____

Notes

Beyond Forgiveness – A Place of Greater Blessing

"is not provoked, thinks no evil;" 1 Corinthians 13:5c "

I confess to being somewhat of a hot-head. It's not something I am proud of; it is an area of my life I am working very hard at. I often have to apologize for the occasional rant. I have to be particularly careful because my hatred of injustice, frustration over disorganization of any kind, and intolerance for corruption can cause an outburst, sometimes without knowing all of the facts *(okay - sometimes I do have all of the facts, but it's still not right).* I have offended people here in Croatia with my occasional rant about one system or another that I felt was not operating fairly or in an organized manner. I have had to apologize profusely for that, because in those moments I lost my head and forgot that I am not a Croatian citizen and therefore do not have an unlimited right to an opinion and every country has its advantages and disadvantages. To broadcast a country's disadvantages, as I have, isn't fair. Croatian people are proud of their country - as well they should be! Croatia is a very lovely country with a long, rich history! My rants are offensive.

And all of this boils down to an area of Agape love that has been, and still is, a journey for me.

Agape love is not easily provoked

I have heard many Christians use the story of Jesus cleansing the temple of the money changers as an example, or excuse, for their anger over social injustice or church government.

However, let us pause for a moment and remember that we are not Jesus.

Jesus was God and therefore would not have sinned in his anger. We are 100% human and have a great propensity to sin in our anger. In fact, I would venture to say that 99% of the time we sin in our anger because anger is a powerful feeling that left unchecked leads to bitterness, hate, and a desire for revenge. A vast majority of the time we manage to fool ourselves into thinking that we are responding in righteous anger. But *"The heart [is] deceitful above all [things], And desperately wicked; who can know it?" (Jeremiah 17:9)*

Above all - Paul instructs us that Agape love is not easily provoked. When we are filled up with the pure love of Jesus there is very little room for anger and we have a greater ability to grace others and give people the benefit of the doubt.

And this is much needed in the body of Christ. As believers we tend to extend very little grace to one another - especially in smaller congregations. We tend to have higher expectations of our brothers and sisters in Christ than we do for ourselves - or we extend a greater measure grace to ourselves than we do to them. Our failure to extend grace to one another causes riffs, cliques, distrust, church splits, and an overall heavy atmosphere in the body.

However, a church that knows how to extend grace and love is a church that allows the body to be open and trusting, genuine and sincere without fear of judgment or condemnation. That open trust, and lack of fear combined with grace, enables God's work to flow unhindered.

Paul goes on to tell us that *agape love thinks no evil*. Other translations say "keeps no record of wrongs". Both are accurate. In other words - we must control our thoughts. So much of our outward expression of anger results from a mind that continually rehashes and rehearses old hurts. There is another word for this: unforgiveness. The danger in unforgiveness is that when we refuse to forgive we forfeit our ability to be forgiven by God. *That's a dangerous place to be!*

Jesus said, *"But if you do not forgive men their trespasses, neither will your Father forgive your trespasses. "* Matthew 6:15

Unforgiveness is literally placing ourselves on the throne of our own lives, assuming God's position, and saying, "God may forgive you of the wrong you committed, but I will not!" It is the ultimate display of pride!

Agape love chooses to forgive *and* forget. It *chooses* to never dwell on the offense ever again. Every time the offense comes to mind, Agape love releases it back to the Lord and replaces the thought with God's love.

But Agape love takes this a step further. Agape love makes the choice to think the best of the one who wronged her. It makes the choice never to listen to a negative word about the one who wronged her It makes the choice to genuinely want the best for the one who wronged her.

Dear reader - All of us have experienced offense in our lives and have been presented with the choice to forgive or entertain bitterness. If you have made the latter choice, please take some time today to pray and allow God's grace to enable you to forgive the one who offended you. Then, begin taking steps to releasing all anger by replacing those angry thoughts with scriptures of God's love. Pray blessings over your offender, and cry out to God for Him to fill you with His Agape love. Are you easily provoked, perhaps you have a hidden area of bitterness that you have not released, or perhaps you just need to invite a greater measure of God's love and peace into your heart.

Day 7 Study Materials

Write out today's verse *1 Corinthians 13:5c:*

_____

_____

_____

_____

_____

Write down the keywords in this verse:

_____   _____

_____   _____

_____   _____

_____   _____

_____   _____

_____   _____

What does this verse mean for your personal life right now? In what way can you put it to practical use?

_____

_____

_____

_____

_____

Describe a time recently when you were provoked.

_____

_____

_____

_____

_____

What triggered the anger in you that caused you to become provoked?

_____

_____

_____

How could you have responded differently so that God's grace would have been released through you, instead of anger?

_____

_____

_____

_____

_____

Are there people whom you have yet not forgiven? _____

Forgiveness does not validate wrong behavior; it simply removes us from the throne of our lives. It frees us to allow God to be the Lord of our lives and do in our hearts what He has destined all along. What steps do you need to take today toward forgiveness of those who have wronged you?

_____

_____

_____

Notes

Don't Shoot the Wounded

"does not rejoice in iniquity, but rejoices in the truth;" 1 Corinthians 13:6

We've all be the victim *and* participant. You know: the whispering and *gasp* "No! Really? She did *that???"*

At one time or another we've all secretly hoped someone would fail at something we didn't agree with, learn their lesson, or "get theirs".

Agape love doesn't not rejoice in iniquity.

Gossip is literally rejoicing in iniquity. It enjoys the thrill of passing on a bad report about someone else. It loves the reaction from the other listener, and it feeds on the slander that soils and destroys that person's reputation. The evil and bitter desire for another's failure and disappointment is deeply rooted in bitterness and pride. It comes directly from the evil one who seeks to destroy the work of God and render it completely ineffective. Both are a deadly cancer that is eating churches alive all over the world.

We see this clearly among congregations that fight and bicker amongst themselves - forgetting who their true enemy is! And Satan sits back and enjoys the show, because he has succeeded in shifting our focus off of him as we engage in civil warfare with one another. It is wrong!

True love, God's love, never rejoices in the downfall of a brother or sister! God's love never wishes failure on His children. God's love will not listen to, or engage in, gossip – *ever*; because it rejoices in truth that God loves *all* mankind. His desire is for us to succeed, to win, and to be the best we can be! Are there times when we fail? Sure. But He is there to pick us up, dust us off, and help us move forward toward prize!

I love how God included stories of Moses' anger, Abraham's lies, and David's infidelity; Rahab the harlot - who was in Jesus' bloodline, Jonah's self-righteousness, Peter's betrayal, and Paul's estrangement from fellow minister John Mark. We see that though we stand among giants, they also had feet of clay. They were not perfect. It reminds us that we are all capable of great failure and are in need of the grace of God. But it also reminds us that our brothers and sisters are also capable of great failure and need His grace, too. And one way God chooses to extend grace to them is through us.

Rejoice in the truth!

Rejoice in the good reports.

Rejoice in the positive attributes of your brothers and sisters.

Rejoice in the successes of the congregation across town.

Rejoice in the fact that God's grace extends far beyond what we can imagine.

And when you see a brother or sister fall run to his side, help him to his feet, dust him off, and encourage him in the grace of the Lord. But above all - do not share his failure with another and do not rejoice in his iniquity. ***Do not shoot your wounded.***

Day 8 Study Materials

Write out today's verse *1 Corinthians 13:6:*

_____

_____

_____

_____

_____

Write down the keywords in this verse:

_____   _____

_____   _____

_____   _____

_____   _____

_____   _____

_____

What does this verse mean for your personal life right now? In what way can you put it to practical use?

_____

_____

_____

_____

_____

List five things you like about your pastor

_____

_____

_____

_____

_____

List five things you like about your local church

_____

_____

_____

_____

_____

Write out Philippians 4:8

_____

_____

_____

_____

_____

Is there a struggling or difficult brother or sister in your local body? _____

Using the attributes of Philippians 4:8, write down one positive thing about that person for each attribute and then thank God for that person as you rejoice in good.

_____

_____

_____

Describe one way you can reach out to this person to show them the love and grace of Jesus Christ

Notes

A Hollywood Love

"bears all things, believes all things, hopes all things, endures all things." 1 Corinthians 13:7

Today's generation truly suffers from a gross misconception of what love is. In every sense: romantic love, familial love, friendship love, and a general caring for mankind.

Our world is crippled with divorce, estranged family members, broken friendships, and neighbors who have never met. I could write all day long about the stories we read in the news: but there is nothing more telling than those of bullying and young people killing their peers.

There is a serious lack of true love because our world is dangerously destitute spiritually. We cannot have God's love in our hearts if He is not living in us. This is why a part of loving is caring for the lost - and a church is never more effective than when she is looking outward! Reaching outward! Focused on her mission!

However, what is even more disturbing is when we see this same lack of love in the church: the same kind of divorce, estrangement in families, broken friendships and a lack of concern for our brothers and sisters in Christ. *That* is very alarming! As God's children, we are responsible to be the ones to show His love to the world. Yet we fail to show His love in our own homes and churches!

Perhaps we are so filled with what the world perceives love to be - what Hollywood and the media portray love to be - that we have forgotten that

Love is not a feeling

Love is a willful choice

Love must be maintained

Love must sometimes be fought for

Love requires endurance

Paul says that love *bears, believes, hopes, and endures **all things.*** We all know this verse. But how many of your have stopped to ponder it?

Bear all things. Do you bear all things with your children, husband, siblings, and church family? Or are you quick to get angry and tell them what you think?

Believe all things. Are you quick to criticize and jump to conclusions? Or are you the one who chooses to believe the best about each person you meet - giving them the benefit of the doubt until they are proven guilty?

Hope all things. When a brother or sister falls, do you maintain hope for them? Or are you quick to write them off as backslidden? Do you reach out a hand to help them back on their feet and refuse to let them fall behind, or do you shrug your shoulders and say, "I saw that coming! I knew they wouldn't stay around."

Endure all things. Are you willing to battle for a friendship, marriage, your children, your family members? Do you refuse to let them slip away from you? Or are you quick to write people off? Is your "blacklist" filled with names of exes and formers?

We live in a very temporary, momentary, fickle, and instant society where we toss what we don't like, and move on to the next best thing. Sadly, this has cropped up in the area of relationships. But there is no room for temporary, momentary, fickle and instant ideas in God's kingdom! He is a God who never changes, never fails, and never forsakes. He never gives up on us. And as His church, we are responsible to show this same kind of enduring love to the world. We do that best when we first start at home and in our local congregations.

Dear reader - have you been guilty of Hollywood love? Have you been quick to write people off and move on? Perhaps now is the right time to make that right. Grab the phone, write a letter, send an email, and let those people know that you are working on building true Agape love in your life - and you want to start with them! Today! Right now. Don't let another moment pass without reaching out.

Day 9 Study Materials

Write out today's verse *1 Corinthians 13:7:*

_____

_____

_____

_____

_____

Write down the keywords in this verse:

_____   _____

_____   _____

_____   _____

_____   _____

_____   _____

_____   _____

What does this verse mean for your personal life right now? In what way can you put it to practical use?

_____

_____

_____

_____

_____

On a scale of 1-10, how well does your local church display the kind of love we've seen so far in 1 Corinthians 13? _____

In what way can you bear all things in your local church?

_____

_____

_____

_____

In what way can your actions display to your brothers and sisters in Christ that you believe all things?

_____

_____

_____

_____

In what way can you begin to actively hope all things about your local church?

_____

_____

_____

_____

Describe a current situation in which you must endure all things with your local church or a brother and sister in Christ.

_____

_____

_____

Notes

Does not behave rudely,

1 Corinthians 13:5a

Does not seek its own,

1 Corinthians 13:5b

Is not provoked, thinks no evil

1 Corinthians 13:5c

Does not rejoice in iniquity, but rejoices in the truth;

1 Corinthians 13:6

Bears all things, believes all things, hopes all things, endures all things.

1 Corinthians 13:7

God's Eternal Fountain of Perfect Love

"Love never fails. But whether [there are] prophecies, they will fail; whether [there are] tongues, they will cease; whether [there is] knowledge, it will vanish away. For we know in part and we prophesy in part. But when that which is perfect has come, then that which is in part will be done away. " 1 Corinthians 13:8-10

Love never fails. Have you ever contemplated that? Love never fails. But not the Hollywood kind, not the emotional kind that you felt on your first date. Agape love isn't based on emotion. It isn't familial or a kind feeling you have toward a friend or neighbor. Emotions change and are often dependent upon situations and circumstances. Familial love and friendship can wan when conflict arises, but Agape love is different. It is perfect. It is eternal. It never fails.

Agape love has nothing to do with our emotions and it remains strong despite distance, conflict, circumstance or situation. Why? Because it is God's love and God never fails.

Many churches place great importance on many things, but fail in the area of Agape love.

Prophesies will fail because we are human and do not always see things clearly. Many a good man - even true a prophet - thought he had heard from the Lord and yet missed the target. We are not perfect yet. Prophesies will fail.

Tongues will cease. One day we will get to heaven and no longer need to use a heavenly language to pray because we will be perfected and know the mind of the Spirit!

Knowledge will vanish as we arrive in Heaven; all things will be suddenly clear to us. But until then we are temporal beings. We rely on past experiences and present situations to arrive at certain conclusions. At times those conclusions are accurate, many times they are not because "we know in part and prophesy in part".

This is why it is so *very* important that we are quick to love, slow to judge and slow to anger. Sadly, it is rare that we see this evident among the people of God - but before we point a finger at this or that congregation, let us remember that even in *this* we are not perfect.

God is perfect and He longs for His perfect love to flow through us to our brothers and sisters in Christ and a world in need. Yet, He chooses to use flawed vessels to pour out that love. While it would be ideal for every church to display every aspect of Agape love exactly as it is described in 1 Corinthians 13, what is reality is that we are apt to fail. This is where we must rely on God's grace to pick up where we fall!

Let us not allow our imperfections to become an excuse for not trying. Even so, let us not be too hard on ourselves and our brothers and sisters in Christ when we fail to display love as we ought. One day, all of what we perceive, know, conclude, judge and discern will come to an end.

But God's perfect love never will!

This is why all we do for Christ must spring from the eternal fountain of His perfect love!

Day 10 Study Materials

Write out today's verse *1 Corinthians 13:8-10:*

_____

_____

_____

_____

_____

Write down the keywords in this verse:

_____   _____

_____   _____

_____   _____

_____   _____

_____   _____

_____   _____

What does this verse mean for your personal life right now? In what way can you put it to practical use?

_____

_____

_____

_____

_____

What does the term "love never fails" mean to you?

_____

_____

_____

_____

Are you able to look past the failures of your pastor, local church and individual brothers and sisters, as you rely on God's grace to remind you that we all see in part and prophesy in part? _____

What does it mean to you to see in part?

_____

_____

_____

_____

_____

How does knowing that we all see in part change your approach to the body of Christ when there are disappointments, failures or disagreements?

_____

_____

_____

_____

_____

Notes

Maturing As God's Kids

"When I was a child, I spoke as a child, I understood as a child, I thought as a child; but when I became a man, I put away childish things." 1 Corinthians 13:11

If there is one thing we have realized in digging through these first 10 verses of 1 Corinthians 13, it is that this special kind of love, Agape love, must be learned.

It is not genetic.

It is not imparted by the laying on of hands.

It is not a free gift - as salvation is.

It is a discipline that must be learned and practiced every day for the rest of our lives. This requires maturity and maturity requires discipline. They go hand in hand.

The best time to start learning and teaching Agape love is from the earliest age possible.

I always find it rather amusing when a parent tries to convince me that children truly *want* to be good, or that their child was so good that they didn't need much discipline. I find it amusing because the Bible says just the opposite. We are all born sinful creatures, from the moment we enter the world we are in dire need of a Savior!

And there is no greater evidence of this fact that a child who has entered toddlerhood with shouts of "no!", temper-tantrums, and other physical displays of rebellion, defiance and anger. And parents sit back in utter amazement while wondering, "Where did he learn that?" He didn't have to *learn* that - it was already there inside of him when he was born.

What a child *must* learn is proper behavior. A child doesn't learn to be selfish, but he *must* learn to share. A child doesn't learn to throw temper-tantrums, but he *must* learn to control his emotions. A child doesn't learn to spit his food out, but he *must* learn to eat what is set before him.

In the same way, a child must learn to love with God's kind of love. And so must we! *It is just a whole lot easier to learn it as a child than as an adult!* And when we mature as adults, we hope that we have learned better how to employ Agape love in our lives.

Just as it is very unattractive to see an adult behaving as a child *(and sadly, we see that all too often!)*, it is unpleasant to encounter those who choose not to love God's way.

A church that engages in learning to love God's way and disciplines herself to act and think the way agape love demands, is a church that has truly matured.

It is time we put away childish displays of selfish pride and learn to love with agape love. To make the choice to practice agape love is to take the first step in Christian maturity.

Your church needs that and the world needs that!

Day 11 Study Materials

Write out today's verse *1 Corinthians 13:11:*

_____

_____

_____

_____

_____

Write down the keywords in this verse:

_____   _____

_____   _____

_____   _____

_____   _____

_____   _____

_____   _____

What does this verse mean for your personal life right now? In what way can you put it to practical use?

_____

_____

_____

_____

_____

List 3 ways you can begin learning to love with Agape love?

_____

_____

_____

How does knowing that we grow into God's love as we mature in Christ help you view the body of Christ differently?

_____

_____

_____

_____

_____

Write out Galatians 5:22-23 below

_____

_____

_____

_____

_____

When we realize that fruit trees – as opposed to other kinds of vegetation – takes years to start bearing fruit, we should understand that God's grace we needed in abundant measure as we seek to live in harmony with our brothers and sisters in Christ. Share your thoughts about this below

_____

_____

_____

_____

_____

Notes

Perception of a Distorted Reflection

"For now we see in a mirror, dimly, but then face to face. Now I know in part, but then I shall know just as I also am known." 1 Corinthians 13:12

Few things break my heart as much as watching churches fight and bicker amongst themselves and engage in conflict with other congregations.

Playing the game of: Anything you can do, I can do better.

Ripping each other apart theologically.

Labeling each other with derogatory labels.

Gossip

Slander

And so much of it boils down to perception.

We hear a 2nd hand story from someone who used to attend a certain congregation, but for whatever reason left and now they pass the bitter taste they were left with on to others. Sadly, few take the time needed to check out the facts. And they assume they know fully the situation.

We find out that the church across town is hosting or participating in a certain project and we begin to form opinions about how its run, what their motives are and how it will eventually turn out in the end. We assume we know fully all of the facts.

A brother or sister makes a certain comment or statement that, for whatever reason, didn't sit well with us and we begin to formulate an opinion about that person without pausing to first consider that perhaps they misspoke or perhaps we didn't understand what they were trying to say - we assume we know fully what they were thinking and what the intentions of their heart were.

But Paul warns that life is like a cloudy mirror. We look into it and all we see is a blurred, distorted and cloudy reflection. One day we will get to heaven and know fully what we only partially know now. That is the hope we have! Perhaps we don't know the whole story - but God does and one day He will make it all clear to us. Until then, let us be great extenders of God's love and grace to His body in every situation.

Let us be the *first* to give grace.

Let us love *fiercely* and *freely*.

If we must err, let us err in believing the **best** about others.

And let us remember that perception is a distorted reflection of what is real. So, before we make a judgment call, obtain facts from the original source and then take them to the One who sees everything with crystal clear clarity!

Day 12 Study Materials

Write out today's verse *1 Corinthians 13:12:*

_____

_____

_____

_____

_____

Write down the keywords in this verse:

_____   _____

_____   _____

_____   _____

_____   _____

_____   _____

What does this verse mean for your personal life right now? In what way can you put it to practical use?

_____

_____

_____

_____

_____

Describe a time when you reacted to a situation, statement, or piece of gossip based on your own perception, only to find out later that you were wrong.

_____

_____

_____

_____

_____

What did you learn from this?

_____

_____

_____

List 3 ways you can remind yourself that your perception is often distorted and to pause before your react?

_____

_____

_____

How do you think the body of Christ would function differently if we would remember not to react hastily, because we don't always see the whole picture or know the whole story?

_____

_____

_____

_____

_____

How dces this factor in with God's grace?

_____

_____

_____

Notes

Invest In Eternity

"And now abide faith, hope, love, these three; but the greatest of these [is] love." 1 Corinthians 13:13

When all is said and done, the message of 1 Corinthians 13 can be reduced to three attributes: *faith, hope, love.*

Faith in our brothers and sisters in Christ, the ones God gave us to walk this narrow path by our side.

Hope in their future and the finishing work God is doing in their lives.

Love for the body of Christ that never gives up, but chooses to believe the best, hope for the best and *do* the best to help them be better today than they were yesterday.

But let's take these three elements to the next level.

"Now faith is the substance of things hoped for, the evidence of things not seen." Hebrews 11:1

Faith is what enables us to believe that what we merely hope for, and what we cannot yet see, *will* one day be reality.

Hope is looking to our future with expectancy and anticipation.

Yet, one day faith will fade away as we are finally able to clearly see. And all that we hoped for and anticipated will become reality. And all that is left is love.

Love.

God is love.

John reminded us of this over and over in the book 1 John. God *is* love. It is His character - the very essence of His being. And this is what makes Him so far above what we can fathom, because while God is holy, righteous and just - He is also love. His character is the perfect balance of principle and grace. Holiness and love. Righteousness and love. Justice and love.

If the very essence of God isn't love then He would never have released His Son to come to earth and die for the sins of those who spit in His face, trampled His law, and prostituted themselves with other gods. What other motivation could there be to sacrifice something as precious as your only child than pure, unadulterated love? And what is amazing is that He uses *us* - flawed, broken vessels - to communicate that love to mankind. He trusts us with this beautiful gift, to show the world the essence of Himself through the prism of a love we can barely comprehend ourselves. And the best way to communicate it effectively is to become as much like His as a mortal can.

Spend regular time in His presence

Know His Word

Let Him to show you areas where you fall short of His grace

Allow His light to illuminate every part of your being.

Because one day faith and hope will fade away, but love is eternal.

Invest in eternity!

Day 13 Study Materials

Write out today's verse *1 Corinthians 13:13:*

_____

_____

_____

_____

_____

Write down the keywords in this verse:

_____   _____

_____   _____

_____   _____

_____   _____

_____   _____

What does this verse mean for your personal life right now? In what way can you put it to practical use?

_____

_____

_____

_____

_____

Define faith.

_____

_____

_____

Define hope.

_____

_____

_____

Define love.

_____

_____

_____

Why do you think Paul says the greatest of these is love?

_____

_____

_____

Why not faith – since we are saved by faith?

_____

_____

_____

What does the statement "the greatest of these is love" mean for the body of Christ and our relationship as a spiritual family?

_____

_____

_____

Notes

A Fervent Holy Zeal

"To the angel of the church of Ephesus write, 'These things says He who holds the seven stars in His right hand, who walks in the midst of the seven golden lampstands: I know your works, your labor, your patience, and that you cannot bear those who are evil. And you have tested those who say they are apostles and are not, and have found them liars; and you have persevered and have patience, and have labored for My name's sake and have not become weary. Nevertheless I have [this] against you, that you have left your first love. Remember therefore from where you have fallen; repent and do the first works, or else I will come to you quickly and remove your lampstand from its place--unless you repent." Revelation 2:1-5

It was a solid church. The members were faithful, patient, discerning, and very careful to search the scriptures. They had persevered in the face of evil and persecution. They were hard workers for the kingdom of God, and did not grow weary in well doing. They were active. In fact, they even displayed a righteous and holy hatred for a group of so-called believers who believed they had special freedoms to engage in immorality and idolatry. In other words, they were dedicated to biblical principles and upheld righteousness, holiness and purity. However, in all of their dedication to the kingdom; to holiness, righteousness and the principles of the Word of God, they left out one thing:

Love

God feels so strongly about this that He even tells the church of Ephesus that if they fail in the following three areas He will literally remove their lampstand.

The three things He commanded them to do were:

Confess that they were a fallen church

Repent of their lack of love

Go back and repeat their first works again (exhibit the zeal they once had, but lost when they grew religious in their duties)

What did the lampstand represent?

Their light in a dark world. The presence and anointing of God; without which they would cease to be effective at all or relevant to the people they were ministering to.

This is a great danger for any church. Especially for churches that are extremely dedicated to evangelism and discipleship. They have great vision, strong dedication, a passion to reach the lost, and a burning desire to carry the gospel to world. However, in all of their dedication and hard work, they fail to stoke the fires of their own hearts; they become so busy *doing* the work of the ministry that they fail to allow the Holy Spirit to keep the fire of love burning in their hearts. After a while they burn out, but their dedication to the ministry prevents them from giving up, so they continue to labor out of religious duty and not love or zeal for the Lord.

And this is exactly the place where enemy wants the church of God to be for 3 reasons.

1. *Religious duty is void of the power of God.*
If we truly want to be effective ministers, we have to have the power of God moving in our hearts. If we do not have the power of God fueling our ministry, then we can accurately say that we are ministering in our own strength.

We cannot minister in might nor power, but only by the Spirit! Furthermore, if the Lord is not building the house *(anointing our ministry)* then we are laboring in vain.

2. *Ministry without love is useless.*
We have looked extensively at the fact that all we do for the Lord and our relationship with the body must flow from the fountain of love. If it doesn't, all we do for the Lord is useless, irritating, and amounts to nothing.

God is love and so if we are not operating and ministering in love, and if our ministry is motivated by anything other than love, then we are ministering out of useless religiosity.

3. *Religious service void of the love of God will not be blessed.*
God's message to the church of Ephesus was clear: confess your fallen state, repent, and return to your former zeal - return to your first love - or your light will be snuffed out and your ministry rendered ineffective.

If we want to be a blessed and effective church we must have the love of God at the center of all we do. If we are not motivated by love, we may continue to do the work of ministry, but it will not be blessed by Him, it will not be effective for His kingdom, and we will fail to bring His light to bear in a darkened world.

Have you forsaken your first love? Has your labor for Him become a religious duty? Have you lost your zeal for the Lord?

Take heart! There is a way back to your First Love.

Take some time over the next month to fast and pray. Set aside blocks of time where you can rise early or stay up late so you can spend time in the presence of Jehovah allowing Him to stoke the fires of your heart!

Read the Bible for *you* - not for ministry. All the Lord to speak to you, rather than only *through* you. And ask the Holy Spirit to refresh and fill you once again.

Then purpose to continue doing this on a daily basis.

In order to minister we must be ministered to. We must allow the Holy Spirit to regularly keep us fueled with His love, which happens only in His presence; in the Holy Place where He dwells and where He wants us to dwell with Him.

When we continually dwell in that secret place - that holy place - we can be sure that all we do and say will be saturated with His love and our service for Him will be fueled by a fervent holy zeal for His kingdom!

And our ministry will flow from the fountain of First Love!

Day 14 Study Materials

Write out today's verse *Revelation 2:1-5:*

_____

_____

_____

_____

_____

Write down the keywords in this verse:

_____   _____

_____   _____

_____   _____

_____   _____

_____   _____

_____   _____

What does this verse mean for your personal life right now? In what way can you put it to practical use?

_____

_____

_____

_____

_____

List the positive qualities of the Ephesus.

_____

_____

_____

_____

What does the statement "left your first love" mean?

_____

_____

_____

_____

As you look at your own life, do you feel you have left your first love – or has there been a time when this was true for you? Describe

_____

_____

_____

_____

How can a church – and individual Christians – prevent this from happening?

_____

_____

_____

What kind of impact does a church who has lost her first love have on the world around her?

_____

_____

_____

_____

How does this letter written to the church in Ephesus fit in the context of 1 Corinthians 13?

_____

_____

_____

_____

_____

In what way has this study impacted your perception of the local church and the role you play in it?

_____

_____

_____

_____

_____

Notes

Love never fails. But whether there are prophecies, they will fail; whether there are tongues, they will cease; whether there is knowledge, it will vanish away. For we know in part and we prophesy in part. But when that which is perfect has come, then that which is in part will be done away.

1 Corinthians 13:8-10

When I was a child, I spoke as a child, I understood as a child, I thought as a child; but when I became a man, I put away childish things.

1 Corinthians 13:11

For now we see in a mirror, dimly, but then face to face. Now I know in part, but then I shall know just as I also am known.

1 Corinthians 13:12

And now abide faith, hope, love, these three; but the greatest of these is love

1 Corinthians 13:13

To the angel of the church of Ephesus write, 'These things says He who holds the seven stars in His right hand, who walks in the midst of the seven golden lampstands: I know your works, your labor, your patience, and that you cannot bear those who are evil. And you have tested those who say they are apostles and are not, and have found them liars; and you have persevered and have patience, and have labored for My name's sake and have not become weary. Nevertheless I have this against you, that you have left your first love. Remember therefore from where you have fallen; repent and do the first works, or else I will come to you quickly and remove your lampstand from its place--unless you repent.

Revelation 2:1-5